The Exploits of the Incompar
Mulla Nasrudin

The Exploits of the Incomparable MULLA NaSRuDin

by
IDRIES SHAH
drawings by
RichaRD WilliamS

A Dutton **dep** Paperback

New York: E. P. Dutton & Co., Inc. 1972

This paperback edition of
"The Exploits of the Incomparable Mulla Nasrudin"
First published 1972 by E. P. Dutton & Co., Inc.
All rights reserved. Printed in the U.S.A.

First Edition

Text and illustrations copyright © 1966
by Mulla Nasrudin Enterprises Ltd.

SBN 0-525-47339-4

Contents

Introduction

MANY countries claim Mulla Nasrudin as a native, though few have gone so far as Turkey in exhibiting his grave and holding an annual Nasrudin Festival, when people dress up and enact the famous jokes at Eskishehr, the reputed place of his birth.

The Greeks, who adopted few things from the Turks, regard Nasrudin quips as part of their own folklore. In the Middle Ages Nasrudin tales were widely used to deride odious authority. In more recent times, the Mulla became a People's Hero of the Soviet Union, when a film depicted him as scoring again and again off the wicked capitalist rulers of the country.

Nasrudin shades off into the Arab figure of Joha, and reappears in the folklore of Sicily. Stories attributed in Central Asia to the corpus are found applied to Baldakiev in Russia, in *Don Quixote*, even in the oldest French book, the *Fables* of Marie de France.

The Mulla is variously referred to as very stupid, improbably clever, the possessor of mystical secrets. The dervishes use him as a figure to illustrate, in their teachings, the antics characteristic of the human mind. Such is the resilience of Nasrudin that republican Turkey, where the dervish orders were suppressed forty years ago, publishes booklets about him as part of their tourist activity.

Scholars have used a great deal of ink on Nasrudin, though traditionally he had little time for them. Because the Mulla is reported to have said, 'I am upside down in this life', some have gone so far as to invert the reputed date of his death, trying to find the truth about the matter.

The Sufis, who believe that deep intuition is the only real guide to knowledge, use these stories almost like exercises. They ask people to choose a few which especially appeal to them, and to turn them over in the mind, making them their own. Teaching masters of the dervishes say that in this way a breakthrough into a higher wisdom can be effected.

But the Sufis concur with those who are not following a mystic way that everyone can do with the Nasrudin tales what people have done through the centuries – enjoy them.

IDRIES SHAH

'Mulla Nasrudin, Chief of the Dervishes and Master of a hidden treasure, a perfected man... Many say: I wanted to learn, but here I have found only madness. Yet, should they seek deep wisdom elsewhere, they may not find it.'

(from *Teachings of Nasrudin*, Bokharan MS. of 1617, by Ablahi Mutlaq, 'The Utter Idiot')

The Exploits of the Incomparable
Mulla Nasrudin

The Alternative

'I am a hospitable man,' said Nasrudin to a group of cronies at the teahouse.

'Very well, then — take us all home to supper,' said the greediest.

Nasrudin collected the whole crowd and started towards his house with them.

When he was almost there, he said:

'I'll go ahead and warn my wife: you just wait here.'

His wife cuffed him when he told her the news. 'There is no food in the house — turn them away.'

'I can't do that, my reputation for hospitality is at stake.'

'Very well, you go upstairs and I'll tell them that you are out.'

After nearly an hour the guests became restless and crowded round the door, shouting, 'Let us in, Nasrudin.'

The Mulla's wife went out to them.

'Nasrudin is out.'

'But we saw him go into the house, and we have been watching the door all the time.'

She was silent.

The Mulla, watching from an upstairs window, was unable to contain himself. Leaning out he shouted: 'I could have gone out by the back door, couldn't I?'

Why we are here

Walking one evening along a deserted road, Mulla Nasrudin saw a troop of horsemen coming towards him.

His imagination started to work; he saw himself captured and sold as a slave, or impressed into the army.

Nasrudin bolted, climbed a wall into a graveyard, and lay down in an open tomb.

Puzzled at his strange behaviour, the men — honest travellers — followed him.

They found him stretched out, tense and quivering.

'What are you doing in that grave? We saw you run away. Can we help you?'

'Just because you can ask a question does not mean that there is a straightforward answer to it,' said the Mulla, who now realized what had happened. 'It all depends upon your viewpoint. If you must know, however: *I* am here because of *you*, and *you* are here because of *me*.'

Never know when it might come in useful

asrudin sometimes took people for trips in his boat One day a fussy pedagogue hired him to ferry him across a very wide river.

As soon as they were afloat the scholar asked whether it was going to be rough.

'Don't ask me nothing about it,' said Nasrudin.

'Have you never studied grammar?'

'No,' said the Mulla.

'In that case, half your life has been wasted.'

The Mulla said nothing.

Soon a terrible storm blew up. The Mulla's crazy cockleshell was filling with water.

He leaned over towards his companion.

'Have you ever learnt to swim?'

'No,' said the pedant.

'In that case, schoolmaster, ALL your life is lost, for we are sinking.

See what I mean?

Nasrudin was throwing handfuls of crumbs around his house.

'What are you doing?' someone asked him.

'Keeping the tigers away.'

'But there are no tigers in these parts.'

'That's right. Effective, isn't it?'

If a Pot can multiply

One day Nasrudin lent his cooking pots to a neighbour, who was giving a feast. The neighbour returned them, together with one extra one — a very tiny pot.

'What is this?' asked Nasrudin.

'According to law, I have given you the offspring of your property which was born when the pots were in my care,' said the joker.

Shortly afterwards Nasrudin borrowed his neighbour's pots, but did not return them.

The man came round to get them back.

'Alas!' said Nasrudin, 'they are dead. We have established, have we not, that pots are mortal?'

The Smuggler

Time and again Nasrudin passed from Persia to Greece on donkey-back. Each time he had two panniers of straw, and trudged back without them. Every time the guard searched him for contraband. They never found any.

'What are you carrying, Nasrudin?'

'I am a smuggler.'

Years later, more and more prosperous in appearance, Nasrudin moved to Egypt. One of the customs men met him there.

'Tell me, Mulla, now that you are out of the jurisdiction of Greece and Persia, living here in such luxury—what was it that you were smuggling when we could never catch you?'

'Donkeys.'

How Nasrudin created Truth

'Laws as such do not make people better,' said Nasrudin to the King; 'they must practise certain things, in order to become attuned to inner truth. This form of truth resembles apparent truth only slightly.'

The King decided that he could, and would, make people observe the truth. He could make them practise truthfulness.

His city was entered by a bridge. On this he built a gallows. The following day, when the gates were opened at dawn, the Captain of the Guard was stationed with a squad of troops to examine all who entered.

An announcement was made: 'Everyone will be questioned. If he tells the truth, he will be allowed to enter. If he lies, he will be hanged.'

Nasrudin stepped forward.

'Where are you going?'

'I am on my way', said Nasrudin slowly, 'to be hanged.'

'We don't believe you!'

'Very well, if I have told a lie, hang me!'

'But if we hang you for lying, we will have made what you said come true!'

'That's right: now you know what truth is — YOUR truth!'

The Cat and the Meat

Nasrudin gave his wife some meat to cook for guests. When the meal arrived, there was no meat. She had eaten it.

'The cat ate it, all three pounds of it,' she said.

Nasrudin put the cat on the scales. It weighed three pounds.

'If this is the cat,' said Nasrudin, 'where is the meat? If, on the other hand, this is the meat—where is the cat?'

There is more Light here

Someone saw Nasrudin searching for something on the ground.

'What have you lost, Mulla?' he asked. 'My key,' said the Mulla. So they both went down on their knees and looked for it.

After a time the other man asked: 'Where exactly did you drop it?'

'In my own house.'

'Then why are you looking here?'

'There is more light here than inside my own house.'

The Fool

A philosopher, having made an appointment to dispute with Nasrudin, called and found him away from home.

Infuriated, he picked up a piece of chalk and wrote 'Stupid Oaf' on Nasrudin's gate.

As soon as he got home and saw this, the Mulla rushed to the philosopher's house.

'I had forgotten', he said, 'that you were to call. And I apologize for not having been at home. Of course, I remembered the appointment as soon as I saw that you had left your name on my door.'

Cooking by Candle

Nasrudin made a wager that he could spend a night on a near-by mountain and survive, in spite of ice and snow. Several wags in the teahouse agreed to adjudicate.

Nasrudin took a book and a candle and sat through the coldest night he had ever known. In the morning, half-dead, he claimed his money.

'Did you have nothing at all to keep you warm?' asked the villagers.

'Nothing.'

'Not even a candle?'

'Yes, I had a candle.'

'Then the bet is off.'

Nasrudin did not argue.

Some months later he invited the same people to a feast at his house. They sat down in his reception room, waiting for the food. Hours passed.

They started to mutter about food.

'Let's go and see how it is getting on,' said Nasrudin.

Everyone trooped into the kitchen. They found an enormous pot of water, under which a candle was burning. The water was not even tepid.

'It is not ready yet,' said the Mulla. 'I don't know why – it has been there since yesterday.'

Danger has no Favourites

A lady brought her small son to the Mulla's school.

'He is very badly behaved,' she explained, 'and I want you to frighten him.'

The Mulla assumed a threatening posture, eyes flaming and face working. He jumped up and down, and suddenly ran out of the building. The woman fainted. When she had come to, she waited for the Mulla, who returned slowly and gravely.

'I asked you to frighten the boy, not me!'

'Dear Madam,' said the Mulla, 'did you not see how afraid I was of myself as well? When danger threatens, it threatens all alike.'

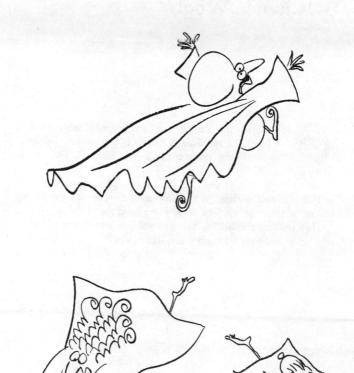

Salt is not Wool

One day the Mulla was taking a donkey-load of salt to market, and drove the ass through a stream. The salt was dissolved. The Mulla was angry at the loss of his load. The ass was frisky with relief.

Next time he passed that way he had a load of wool. After the animal had passed through the stream, the wool was thoroughly soaked, and very heavy. The donkey staggered under the soggy load.

'Ha!' shouted the Mulla, 'you thought you would get off lightly *every* time you went through water, didn't you?'

Can Good Turns be accidental?

Nasrudin's donkey ran towards a pool to drink. The sides were very steep, and it was just about to over-balance and fall in when frogs began to croak loudly from the water.

This so frightened the ass that it reared up, and by this means was able to save itself.

Nasrudin threw a handful of money into the water, crying,

'Frogs, you did me a good turn. Here is something for you to celebrate with.'

The Unsuspected Element

wo men were quarrelling outside Nasrudin's window at dead of night. Nasrudin got up, wrapped his only blanket around himself, and ran out to try to stop the noise.

When he tried to reason with the drunks, one snatched his blanket and both ran away.

'What were they arguing about ?' asked his wife when he went in.

'It must have been the blanket. When they got that, the fight broke up.'

The Burglars

Hearing someone moving about in his house, the Mulla became frightened and hid in a cupboard.

In the course of their search, the two burglars opened the door and saw him cowering there.

'What are you hiding from us?' asked one.

'I am hiding from shame that there is nothing in this house worthy of your attentions.'

Eating-matter and Reading-matter

Nasrudin was carrying home some liver which he had just bought. In the other hand he had a recipe for liver pie which a friend had given him.

Suddenly a buzzard swooped down and carried off the liver.

'You fool!' shouted Nasrudin, 'the meat is all very well – but I still have the recipe!'

Adventures in the Desert

'When I was in the desert,' said Nasrudin one day, 'I caused an entire tribe of horrible and bloodthirsty bedouins to run.'

'However did you do it?'

'Easy. I just ran, and they ran after me.'

Circumstances alter Cases

The rain was pelting down. Aga Akil, the most sanctimonious man in town, was running for shelter. 'How dare you flee from God's bounty,' thundered Nasrudin at him, 'the liquid from Heaven? As a devout man, you should know that rain is a blessing for all creation.'

The Aga was anxious to maintain his reputation. 'I had not thought of it in that way,' he muttered, and slackening his pace he arrived home soaked through. Of course he caught a chill.

Soon afterwards, as he sat wrapped in blankets at his window, he espied Nasrudin pelting through the rain, and challenged him: 'Why are you running away from divine blessings, Nasrudin? How dare you spurn the blessing which it contains?'

'Ah,' said Nasrudin, 'you don't seem to realize that I do not want to defile it with my feet.'

The Food of the Cloak

Nasrudin heard that there was a banquet being held in the near-by town, and that everyone was invited. He made his way there as quickly as he could. When the Master of Ceremonies saw him in his ragged cloak, he seated him in the most inconspicuous place, far from the great table where the most important people were being waited on hand and foot.

Nasrudin saw that it would be an hour at least before the waiters reached the place where he was sitting. So he got up and went home.

He dressed himself in a magnificent sable cloak and turban and returned to the feast. As soon as the heralds of the Emir, his host, saw this splendid sight they started to beat the drum of welcome and sound the trumpets in a manner consonant with a visitor of high rank.

The Chamberlain came out of the palace himself, and conducted the magnificent Nasrudin to a place almost next to the Emir. A dish of wonderful food was immediately placed before him. Without a pause, Nasrudin began to rub handfuls of it into his turban and cloak.

'Your Eminence,' said the prince, 'I am curious as to your eating habits, which are new to me.'

'Nothing special,' said Nasrudin; 'the cloak got me in here, got me the food. Surely it deserves its portion?'

The Sermon of Nasrudin

One day the villagers thought they would play a joke on Nasrudin. As he was supposed to be a holy man of some indefinable sort, they went to him and asked him to preach a sermon in their mosque. He agreed.

When the day came, Nasrudin mounted the pulpit and spoke:

'O people! Do you know what I am going to tell you?'

'No, we do not know,' they cried.

'Until you know, I cannot say. You are too ignorant to make a start on,' said the Mulla, overcome with indignation that such ignorant people should waste his time. He descended from the pulpit and went home.

Slightly chagrined, a deputation went to his house again, and asked him to preach the following Friday, the day of prayer.

Nasrudin started his sermon with the same question as before.

This time the congregation answered, as one man:

'Yes, we know.'

'In that case,' said the Mulla, 'there is no need for me to detain you longer. You may go.' And he returned home.

Having been prevailed upon to preach for the third Friday in succession, he started his address as before:

'Do you know or do you not?'

The congregation was ready.

'Some of us do, and others do not.'

'Excellent,' said Nasrudin, 'then let those who know communicate their knowledge to those who do not.'

And he went home.

His Excellency

By a series of misunderstandings and coincidences, Nasrudin found himself one day in the audience hall of the Emperor of Persia.

The Shahinshah was surrounded by self-seeking nobles, governors of provinces, courtiers and connivers of all kinds. Each was pressing his own claim to be appointed head of the embassy which was soon to set out for India.

The Emperor's patience was at an end, and he raised his head from the importunate mass, mentally invoking the aid of Heaven in his problem as to whom to choose. His eyes lighted upon Mulla Nasrudin.

'This is to be the Ambassador,' he announced; 'so now leave me in peace.'

Nasrudin was given rich clothes, and an enormous chest of rubies, diamonds, emeralds and priceless works of art was entrusted to him: the gift of the Shahinshah to the Great Mogul.

The courtiers, however, were not finished. United for once by this affront to their claims, they decided to encompass the downfall of the Mulla. First they broke into his quarters and stole the jewels, which they divided among themselves, replacing them with earth to make up the weight. Then they called upon Nasrudin, determined to ruin his embassy, to get him into trouble, and in the process to discredit their master as well.

'Congratulations, great Nasrudin,' they said; 'what the Fountain of Wisdom, Peacock of the World, has ordered must be the essence of all wisdom. We therefore hail you. But there are just a couple of points upon which we may be able to advise you, accustomed as we are to the behaviour of diplomatic emissaries.'

'I should be obliged if you would tell me,' said Nasrudin.

'Very well,' said the chief of the intriguers. 'The first thing is that you must be humble. In order to show how modest you are, therefore, you should not show any sign of importance. When you reach India you will enter as many mosques as you can, and make collections for yourself. The second thing is that you must observe Court etiquette in the country to which you are accredited. This will mean that you will refer to the Great Mogul as "the Full Moon".'

'But is that not a title of the Persian Emperor?'

'Not in India.'

So Nasrudin set out. The Persian Emperor told him as they took leave: 'Be careful, Nasrudin. Adhere to etiquette, for the Mogul is a mighty emperor and we must impress him while not affronting him in any way.'

'I am well prepared, Majesty,' said Nasrudin.

As soon as he entered the territory of India, Nasrudin went into a mosque and mounted the pulpit: 'O people!' he cried, 'see in me the representative of the Shadow of Allah upon Earth! The Axis of the Globe! Bring out your money, for I am making a collection.'

This he repeated in every mosque he could find, all the way from Baluchistan to imperial Delhi.

He collected a great deal of money. 'Do with it', the counsellors had said, 'what you will. For it is the product of intuitive growth and bestowal, and as such its use will create its own demand.' All that they wanted to happen was for the Mulla to be exposed to ridicule for collecting money in this 'shameless' manner. 'The holy must live from their holiness,' roared Nasrudin at mosque after mosque. 'I give no account nor do I expect any. To you, money is something to be hoarded, after being sought. You can exchange it for material things. To me, it is a part of a mechanism. I am the representative of a natural force of intuitive growth, bestowal and disbursement.'

Now, as we all know, good often proceeds from apparent evil, and the reverse. Those who thought that Nasrudin was lining his own pockets did not contribute. For some reason, their affairs did not prosper. Those who were considered credulous and gave their money, became in a mysterious way enriched. But to return to our story.

Sitting on the Peacock Throne the Emperor at Delhi studied the

reports which couriers were daily bringing him, describing the progress of the Persian Ambassador. At first he could make no sense out of them. Then he called his council together.

'Gentlemen,' he said, 'this Nasrudin must indeed be a saint or a divinely guided one. Who ever heard of anyone else violating the principle that one does not seek money without a plausible reason, lest a wrong interpretation be placed upon one's motives?'

'May your shadow never grow less,' they replied, 'O Infinite Extension of all Wisdom: we agree. If there are men like this in Persia, we must beware, for their moral ascendancy over our materialistic outlook is plain.'

Then a runner arrived from Persia, with a secret letter in which the Mogul's spies at the imperial Court reported: 'Mulla Nasrudin is a man of no consequence in Persia. He was chosen absolutely at random to be Ambassador. We cannot fathom the reason for the Shahinshah not being more selective.'

The Mogul called his council together: 'Incomparable Birds of Paradise!' he told them, 'a thought has manifested itself to me. The Persian Emperor has chosen a man at random to represent his whole nation. This may mean that he is so confident of the consistent quality of his people that, for him, ANYONE AT ALL IS QUALIFIED TO UNDERTAKE THE DELICATE TASK OF AMBASSADOR TO THE SUBLIME COURT OF DELHI! This indicates the degree of perfection attained, the amazingly infallible intuitive powers cultivated, among them. We must reconsider our desire to invade Persia; for such a people could easily engulf our arms. Their society is organized on a different basis from our own.'

'You are right, Superlative Warrior on the Frontiers!' cried the Indian nobles.

At length, Nasrudin arrived in Delhi. He was riding his old donkey, and was followed by his escort, weighed down by the sacks of money which he had collected in the mosques. The treasure-chest was mounted on an elephant, such was its size and weight.

Nasrudin was met by the Master of Ceremonies at the gate of Delhi. The Emperor was seated with his nobles in an immense courtyard, the Reception Hall of the Ambassadors. This had been so arranged that the entrance was low. As a consequence, ambassadors were always obliged to dismount from their horses and enter the Supreme Presence on foot, giving the impression of supplicants. Only an equal could ride into the presence of an Emperor.

No ambassador had ever arrived astride a donkey, and thus there was nothing to stop Nasrudin trotting straight through the door, and up to the Imperial Dais.

The Indian King and his courtiers exchanged meaningful glances at this act.

Nasrudin blithely dismounted, addressed the King as the 'Full Moon', and called for his treasure-chest to be brought.

When it was opened, and the earth revealed, there was a moment of consternation.

'I had better say nothing,' thought Nasrudin, 'for there is nothing to say which could mitigate this.' So he remained silent.

The Mogul whispered to his Vizier, 'What does this mean? Is this an insult to the Highest Eminence?'

Incapable of believing this, the Vizier thought furiously. Then he provided the interpretation.

'It is a symbolic act, Presence,' he murmured. 'The Ambassador means that he acknowledges *you* as the Master of the Earth. Did he not call you the Full Moon?'

The Mogul relaxed. 'We are content with the offering of the Persian Shahinshah; for we have no need of wealth; and we appreciate the metaphysical subtlety of the message.'

'I have been told to say,' said Nasrudin, remembering the 'essential gift-offering phrase' given him by the intriguers in Persia, 'that this is all we have for Your Majesty.'

'That means that Persia will not yield one further ounce of her soil to us,' whispered the Interpreter of Omens to the King.

'Tell your master that we understand,' smiled the Mogul. 'But there is one other point: If I am the Full Moon, what is the Persian Emperor?'

'He is the New Moon,' said Nasrudin, automatically.

'The Full Moon is more mature and gives more light than the New Moon, which is its junior,' whispered the Court Astrologer to the Mogul.

'We are content,' said the delighted Indian. 'You may return

49

to Persia and tell the New Moon that the Full Moon salutes him.'

The Persian spies at the Court of Delhi immediately sent a complete account of this interchange to the Shahinshah. They added that it was known that the Mogul Emperor had been impressed, and feared to plan war against the Persians because of the activities of Nasrudin.

When the Mulla returned home, the Shahinshah received him in full audience. 'I am more than pleased, friend Nasrudin,' he said, 'at the results of your unorthodox methods. Our country is saved, and this means that there will be no attempt at accounting for the jewels or the collecting in mosques. You are henceforth to be known by the special title of *Safir* — Emissary.'

'But, Your Majesty,' hissed his Vizier, 'this man is guilty of high treason, if not more! We have perfect evidence that he applied one of your titles to the Emperor of India, thus changing his allegiance and bringing one of your magnificent attributes into disrepute.'

'Yes,' thundered the Shahinshah, 'the sages have said wisely that "to every perfection there is an imperfection". Nasrudin! Why did you call me the New Moon?'

'I don't know about protocol,' said Nasrudin; 'but I do know that the Full Moon is about to wane, and the New Moon is still growing, with its greatest glories ahead of it.'

The Emperor's mood changed. 'Seize Anwar, the Grand Vizier,' he roared. 'Mulla! I offer you the position of Grand Vizier!'

'What!' said Nasrudin. 'Could I accept after seeing with my own eyes what happened to my predecessor?'

And what happened to the jewels and treasures which the evil courtiers had usurped from the treasure-chest? That is another story. As the incomparable Nasrudin said: 'Only children and the stupid seek cause-and-effect in the same story.'

Nasrudin and the Wise Men

The philosophers, logicians and doctors of law were drawn up at Court to examine Nasrudin. This was a serious case, because he had admitted going from village to village saying: 'The so-called wise men are ignorant, irresolute and confused.' He was charged with undermining the security of the State.

'You may speak first,' said the King.

'Have paper and pens brought,' said the Mulla.

Paper and pens were brought.

'Give some to each of the first seven savants.'

They were distributed.

'Have them separately write an answer to this question: "What is bread?"'

This was done.

The papers were handed to the King, who read them out:

The first said: 'Bread is a food.'

The second: 'It is flour and water.'

The third: 'A gift of God.'

The fourth: 'Baked dough.'

The fifth: 'Changeable, according to how you mean "bread".'

The sixth: 'A nutritious substance.'

The seventh: 'Nobody really knows.'

'When they decide what bread is,' said Nasrudin, 'it will be possible for them to decide other things. For example, whether I am right or wrong. Can you entrust matters of assessment and judgment to people like this? Is it or is it not strange that they cannot agree about something which they eat each day, yet are unanimous that I am a heretic?'

Judgment

When the Mulla was a judge in his village, a dishevelled figure ran into his court-room, demanding justice.

'I have been ambushed and robbed,' he cried, 'just outside this village. Someone from here must have done it. I demand that you find the culprit. He took my robe, sword, even my boots.'

'Let me see,' said the Mulla, 'did he not take your undershirt, which I see you are still wearing?'

'No he did not.'

'In that case, he was not from this village. Things are done thoroughly here. I cannot investigate your case.'

First Things first

o the Sufi, perhaps the greatest absurdity in life is the way in which people strive for things — such as knowledge — without the basic equipment for acquiring them. They have assumed that all they need is 'two eyes, a nose and a mouth', as Nasrudin says.

In Sufism, a person cannot learn until he is in a state in which he can perceive what he is learning, and what it means.

Nasrudin went one day to a well, in order to teach this point to a disciple who wanted to know 'the truth'. With him he took the disciple and a pitcher.

The Mulla drew a bucket of water, and poured it into his pitcher. Then he drew another, and poured it in. As he was pouring in the third, the disciple could not contain himself any longer:

'Mulla, the water is running out. There is no bottom in that pitcher.'

Nasrudin looked at him indignantly. 'I am trying to *fill* the pitcher. In order to see when it is full, my eyes are fixed upon the *neck*, not the *bottom*. When I see the water rise to the neck, the pitcher will be full. What has the bottom got to do with it? When I am interested in the bottom of the pitcher, then only will I look at it.'

This is why Sufis do not speak about profound things to people who are not prepared to cultivate the power of learning — something which can only be taught by a teacher to someone who is sufficiently enlightened to say: 'Teach me how to learn.'

There is a Sufi saying: 'Ignorance is pride, and pride is ignorance. The man who says, "I don't have to be taught how to learn" is proud and ignorant.' Nasrudin was illustrating, in this story, the identity of these two states, which ordinary human kind considers to be two different things.

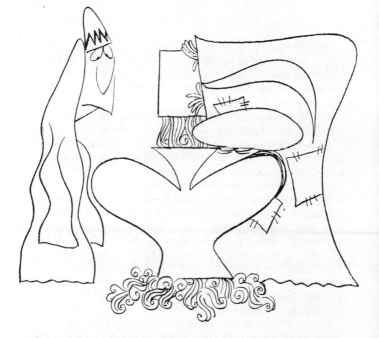

In accordance with the technique known as 'opprobrium', Nasrudin was acting the part of the ignorant man in his pitcher charade.
This is a familiar part of Sufi technique.

His disciple pondered this lesson, linking it with other absurd
actions of the Mulla. A week later he went to Nasrudin and said:
'Teach me about the pitcher. I am now ready to learn.'

Whose Shot was that?

The Fair was in full swing, and Nasrudin's senior disciple asked whether he and his fellow-students might be allowed to visit it.

'Certainly,' said Nasrudin; 'for this is an ideal opportunity to continue practical teaching.'

The Mulla headed straight for the shooting-gallery, one of the great attractions: for large prizes were offered for even one bull's-eye.

At the appearance of the Mulla and his flock the townsfolk gathered around. When Nasrudin himself took up the bow and three arrows, tension mounted. Here, surely, it would be demonstrated that Nasrudin sometimes overreached himself ...

'Study me attentively.' The Mulla flexed the bow, tilted his cap to the back of his head like a soldier, took careful aim and fired. The arrow went very wide of the mark.

There was a roar of derision from the crowd, and Nasrudin's pupils stirred uneasily, muttering to one another. The Mulla turned and faced them all. 'Silence! This was a demonstration of how the soldier shoots. He is often wide of the mark. That is why he loses wars. At the moment when I fired I was identified with a soldier. I said to myself, "I am a soldier, firing at the enemy." '

He picked up the second arrow, slipped it into the bow and tweaked the string. The arrow fell short, halfway towards the target. There was dead silence.

'Now,' said Nasrudin to the company, 'you have seen the shot of a man who was too eager to shoot, yet who, having failed at his first shot, was too nervous to concentrate. The arrow fell short.'

Even the stallholder was fascinated by these explanations. The

Mulla turned nonchalantly towards the target, aimed and let his arrow fly. It hit the very centre of the bull's-eye.

Very deliberately he surveyed the prizes, picked the one which he liked best, and started to walk away. A clamour broke out.

'Silence!' said Nasrudin. 'Let one of you ask me what you all seem to want to know.'

For a moment nobody spoke. Then a yokel shuffled forward. 'We want to know which of you fired the third shot.'

'That? Oh, that was *me*.'

The Magic Bag

A huckster, planning to set up his stall in the market-place, saw Nasrudin coming towards him, counting a handful of coins. He stopped him at once. With any luck he could make a coup.

'You seem like a man of exceptional insight,' he said; 'would you like a magic nosebag?'

'What can it do?'

'Just look and see.'

The conjurer put his hand in the bag and took out first a rabbit, then a ball, finally a growing plant, in a pot. Nasrudin could not give him his money fast enough.

'Just one thing,' said the conjurer, wanting to gain time to get on his way, 'don't annoy it. These bags are temperamental. And don't confide too much in others about this. All will be well in the end.'

Nasrudin had planned to spend the midday rest period in the local teahouse, but he was now so excited that he headed straight for home, bag in hand. By and by it became very hot; he was tired, and thirsty.

The Mulla sat down by the wayside. 'Magic bag,' he said, 'give me a glass of water.'

He put his hand in the bag, but it was empty.

'Ah,' said Nasrudin; 'perhaps it is only giving rabbits, balls and plants, because it is temperamental. He thought it would do no harm to test it.

'All right, then, give me a rabbit.'

No rabbit appeared.

'Don't be annoyed with me, I just don't understand magic bags.' When his donkey was annoyed, he reflected, he bought it a nosebag.

So he rode back to town and bought a donkey for his new nosebag.

'What are you doing with two donkeys?' someone shouted.

'You don't understand,' said the Mulla. 'It is *not* two donkeys. It is one donkey and his nosebag, and one nosebag and his donkey.'

Fear

Nasrudin was walking along a lonely road one moonlit night when he heard a snore, somewhere, it seemed, underfoot. Suddenly he was afraid, and was about to run when he tripped over a dervish lying in a cell which he had dug for himself, partly underground.

'Who are you?' stammered the Mulla.

'I am a dervish, and this is my contemplation-place.'

'You will have to let me share it. Your snore frightened me out of my wits, and I cannot go any further tonight.'

'Take the other end of this blanket, then,' said the dervish without enthusiasm, 'and lie down here. Please be quiet, because I am keeping a vigil. It is a part of a complicated series of exercises. Tomorrow I must change the pattern, and I cannot stand interruption.'

Nasrudin fell asleep for a time. Then he woke up, very thirsty.

'I am thirsty,' he told the dervish.

'Then go back down the road, where there is a stream.'

'No, I am still afraid.'

'I shall go for you, then,' said the dervish. After all, to provide water is a sacred obligation in the East.

'No—don't go. I shall be afraid all by myself.'

'Take this knife to defend yourself with,' said the dervish.

While he was away, Nasrudin frightened himself still more, working himself up into a lather of anxiety, which he tried to counter by imagining how he would attack any fiend who threatened him.

Presently the dervish returned.

'Keep your distance, or I'll kill you!' said Nasrudin.

'But I am the dervish,' said the dervish.

'I don't care who you are—you may be a fiend in disguise. Besides,

you have your head and eyebrows shaved!' The dervishes of that Order shave the head and eyebrows.

'But I have come to bring you water! Don't you remember – you are thirsty!'

'Don't try to ingratiate yourself with me, Fiend!'

'But that is my cell you are occupying!'

'That's hard luck for you, isn't it? You'll just have to find another one.'

'I suppose so,' said the dervish, 'but I am sure I don't know what to make of all this.'

'I can tell you one thing,' said Nasrudin, 'and that is that fear is multidirectional.'

'It certainly seems to be stronger than thirst, or sanity, or other people's property,' said the dervish.

'*And* you don't have to have it yourself in order to suffer from it!' said Nasrudin.

The Robe

Jalal, an old friend of Nasrudin's, called one day. The Mulla said, 'I am delighted to see you after such a long time. I am just about to start on a round of visits, however. Come, walk with me, and we can talk.'

'Lend me a decent robe,' said Jalal, 'because, as you see, I am not dressed for visiting.' Nasrudin lent him a very fine robe.

At the first house Nasrudin presented his friend. 'This is my old companion, Jalal: but the robe he is wearing, that is mine!'

On their way to the next village, Jalal said: 'What a stupid thing to say! "The robe is mine" indeed! Don't do it again.' Nasrudin promised.

When they were comfortably seated at the next house, Nasrudin said: 'This is Jalal, an old friend, come to visit me. But the robe: the robe is *his*!'

As they left, Jalal was just as annoyed as before. 'Why did you say that? Are you crazy?'

'I only wanted to make amends. Now we are quits.'

'If you do not mind,' said Jalal, slowly and carefully, 'we shall not say any more about the robe.' Nasrudin promised.

At the third and final place of call, Nasrudin said: 'May I present Jalal, my friend. And the robe, the robe he is wearing ... But we mustn't say anything about the robe, must we?'

Saved his Life

asrudin, when he was in India, passed near a strange-looking building, at the entrance of which a hermit was sitting. He had an air of abstraction and calm, and Nasrudin thought that he would make some sort of contact with him. 'Surely', he thought, 'a devout philosopher like me must have something in common with this saintly individual.'

'I am a Yogi,' said the anchorite, in answer to the Mulla's question; 'and I am dedicated to the service of all living things, especially birds and fish.'

'Pray allow me to join you,' said the Mulla, 'for, as I had expected, we have something in common. I am strongly attracted to your sentiments, because a fish once saved my life.'

'How pleasurably remarkable!' said the Yogi; 'I shall be delighted to admit you to our company. For all my years of devotion to the cause of animals, I have never yet been privileged to attain such intimate communion with them as you. Saved your life! This amply substantiates our doctrine that all the animal kingdom is interlinked.'

So Nasrudin sat with the Yogi for some weeks, contemplating his navel and learning various curious gymnastics.

At length the Yogi asked him: 'If you feel able, now that we are better acquainted, to communicate to me your supreme experience with the life-saving fish, I would be more than honoured.'

'I am not sure about that,' said the Mulla, 'now that I have heard more of your ideas.'

But the Yogi pressed him, with tears in his eyes, calling him 'Master' and rubbing his forehead in the dust before him.

'Very well, if you insist,' said Nasrudin, 'though I am not quite sure whether you are ready (to use your parlance) for the revelation I have to make. The fish certainly saved my life. I was on the verge of starvation when I caught it. It provided me with food for three days.'

Four-legged

'ause sustenance to be produced for the quadrupeds,' called an affected and imperious nobleman, dismounting in Nasrudin's courtyard, 'and conduct me to the tranquillity-inducing chambers where I may be regaled with appropriate nutriment.'

Such members of the Sultan's Court were difficult to deny, and Nasrudin ran to do his bidding.

When the interloper was settled on the best couch, sipping Nasrudin's coffee, the Mulla brought the Kazi (magistrate) to meet him.

'O great noble,' said Nasrudin, 'have you land?'

'A million jaribs.'

'And do you use quadrupeds for ploughing?'

'Yes, indeed.'

'Would you buy from me two dozen quadrupeds at a price of five silver pieces each?'

The patrician knew plough-animals were worth a hundred pieces of silver. He eagerly assented.

Nasrudin went out and bought twenty-four rabbits for a silver piece each. He presented these quadrupeds to the noble.

He appealed to the Kazi.

'We must stick to the letter of the law,' said the pedant, 'and I uphold the contention that rabbits are four-footed.'

Quiz

here was a great deal of restlessness in the country, and the King had sent a 'cultural delegation' through the villages to reassure people. Everywhere they went the people were most impressed, because between them they marshalled an immense collection of knowledge and expertise.

One was an author, another was a priest, a third was a member of the royal household. There was a lawyer, a soldier and a merchant: and many others. At each place at which they stopped they called a meeting in the nearest open space and people assembled and asked them questions.

When they arrived at Nasrudin's village, a large gathering headed by the Mayor welcomed them. Questions were asked and answered, and everyone was to some degree influenced by the array and importance of the delegation.

Nasrudin arrived late, but as a local celebrity he was pushed forward. 'What are you doing here?' he asked.

The chairman smiled compassionately. 'We are a team of experts, here to answer all the questions that the people cannot answer for themselves. And who, pray, are you?'

'Oh, me,' said Nasrudin offhandedly, 'you'd better have me here, on the platform.' He climbed up beside the dignitaries.

'I am here, you see, to answer the questions which *you* don't know the answers to. Shall we start with some of the things which baffle *you* learned gentlemen?'

The Sign

Nasrudin claimed a knowledge of the stars.

'What Sign were you born under, Mulla?'

'Private Property — Keep Out!'

'No, no, the Sign of the Zodiac.'

'Oh, I see. Well, the Sign of the Donkey.'

'Sign of the Donkey? I don't remember that one.'

'Well, you are older than me. They have had some new ones since your time, you know.'

All her Fault

Nasrudin tried to get a calf into a pen, but it would not go. So he went to its mother and began to reproach her.

'Why are you shouting at that cow?' someone asked.

'It is all her fault,' said Nasrudin, 'for she should have taught him better.'

The Ways of Foreigners

asrudin climbed into an orchard and started to pick apricots. Suddenly the gardener saw him. The Mulla instantly climbed a tree.

'What are you doing here?' the gardener asked.

'Singing. I am a nightingale.'

'All right, nightingale — let me hear you sing.'

Nasrudin warbled a few inharmonious notes, so unlike a bird that the gardener laughed.

'I have never heard that kind of nightingale before,' he said.

'You evidently have not travelled,' said the Mulla. 'I chose the song of a rare, exotic nightingale.'

Burnt Foot

An illiterate came to Nasrudin, and asked him to write a letter for him.

'I can't,' said the Mulla, 'because I have burned my foot.'

'What has that got to do with writing a letter?'

'Since nobody can read my handwriting, I am bound to have to travel somewhere to interpret the letter. And my foot is sore; so there is no point in writing the letter, is there?'

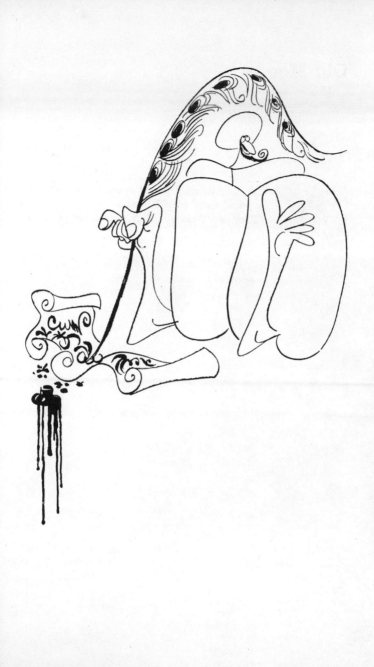

Old Moons

'What do they do with the old moon, when there is a new one?' a wag asked Nasrudin.

'They cut them up. Each old moon provides forty stars.'

Letter of the Law

asrudin found a valuable ring in the street. He wanted to keep it. But according to law the finder of an object had to go to the market-place and shout the fact three times in a loud voice.

At three o'clock in the morning the Mulla went to the square and shouted thrice: 'I have found such-and-such a ring.'

By the third shout, people were pouring into the streets.

'What is it all about, Mulla?' they asked.

'The law lays down a threefold repetition,' said Nasrudin, 'and for all I know I may be breaking it if I say the same thing a fourth time. But I'll tell you something else: I am the owner of a diamond ring all right.'

The Cat is wet

Nasrudin took a job as watchman. His master called him and asked whether it was raining. 'I have to go to see the Sultan, and the dye on my favourite cloak is not fast. If it is raining, it will be ruined.'

Now, Nasrudin was very lazy; and, besides, he prided himself upon being a master of deduction. The cat had just streaked in, soaked through.

'Master,' he said, 'it is raining heavily.'

The master spent some time getting himself arrayed in other finery, went out, and found that there was no rain. The cat had been soaked by someone throwing water at it to scare it away.

Nasrudin got the sack.

Sleep is an Activity

asrudin wanted to steal some fruit from a stall, but the stallholder had a fox which kept watch. He overheard the man say to his fox. 'Foxes are craftier than dogs, and I want you to guard the stall with cunning. There are always thieves about. When you see anyone doing anything, ask yourself why he is doing it, and whether it can be related to the security of the stall.'

When the man had gone away, the fox came to the front of the stall and looked at Nasrudin lurking on a lawn opposite. Nasrudin at once lay down and closed his eyes. The fox thought, 'Sleeping is not *doing* anything.'

As he watched Nasrudin he too began to feel tired. He lay down and went to sleep.

Then Nasrudin crept past him and stole some fruit.

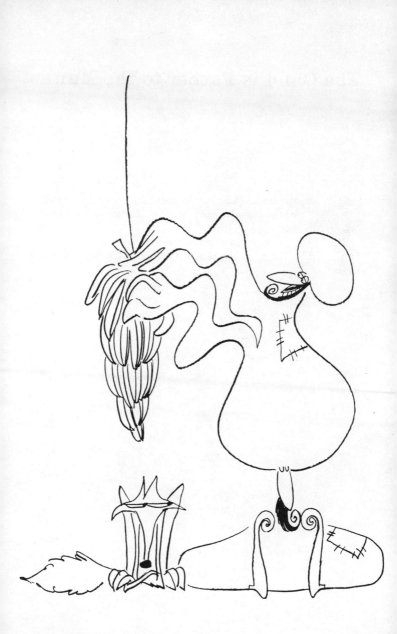

The Child is Father to the Man

Nasrudin arrived at an all-comers' horse-race mounted on the slowest of oxen. Everyone laughed: an ox cannot run.

'But I have seen it, when it was only a calf, running faster than a horse,' said Nasrudin; 'so why should it not run faster, now that it is larger?'

Every little helps

Nasrudin loaded his ass with wood for the fire, and instead of sitting in its saddle, sat astride one of the logs.

'Why don't you sit in the saddle?' someone asked.

'What! and add my weight to what the poor animal has to carry? My weight is on the *wood*, and it is going to stay there.'

Hidden Depths

One day the Mulla was in the market and saw birds for sale at five hundred reals each. 'My bird,' he thought, 'which is larger than any of these, is worth far more.'

The next day he took his pet hen to market. Nobody would offer him more than fifty reals for it. The Mulla began to shout:

'O people! This is a disgrace! Yesterday you were selling birds only half this size at ten times the price.'

Someone interrupted him: 'Nasrudin, those were parrots — talking birds. They are worth more because they talk.'

'Fool!' said Nasrudin; 'those birds you value only because they can talk. This one, which has wonderful thoughts and yet does not annoy people with chatter, you reject.'

Back to Front

Nasrudin was visited by some students, who asked whether they might hear his lessons. He agreed, and they set out towards the lecture-hall, walking behind the Mulla, who had mounted his donkey with his face to its tail.

People began to stare. They thought that the Mulla must be a fool, and the students who followed him even greater fools. Who, after all, walks behind a man who rides a donkey back to front?

After a little while the students began to become uneasy, and said to the Mulla:

'O Mulla! People are looking at us. Why do you ride in this manner?'

Nasrudin frowned. 'You are thinking more about what people think than what we are doing,' he said. 'I shall explain it to you. If you walk in front, this would show disrespect to me, because you would have your backs to me. If I walked behind, the same would be true. If I ride ahead with my back towards you, this shows disrespect for you. This is the only way of doing it.'

Principles of Life-saving

Nasrudin was not sure which of two women he would marry. One day they both cornered him and asked which one he loved the more.

'Put the question in a practical context, and I will try to answer it,' he said.

'If we both fell into the river, which one would you save?' asked the smaller and prettier one.

The Mulla turned to the other, a large but moneyed wench: 'Can you swim, my dear?'

Unsuited

'Take up this sack and carry it to my house,' said Nasrudin to a porter in the market.

'May I be your sacrifice, Effendi. Where is your house?'

The Mulla looked at him aghast. 'You are a disreputable ruffian, and probably a burglar. Do you think that I could ever tell you where my house is?'

Creeping up on himself

Bedar, the Watchman, caught the Mulla prising open the window of his own bedroom from the outside, in the depths of night.

'What are you doing, Nasrudin? Locked out?'

'Hush! They say I walk in my sleep. I am trying to surprise myself and find out.'

His Need is greater than mine

The Mulla one day brought home a cake of soap, and asked his wife to wash his shirt.

No sooner had she started to soap the shirt when a huge crow swooped down, snatched the soap and flew away, perching on a branch.

She gave a furious cry.

The Mulla came running out of the house. 'What happened, my dear?'

'I was just going to wash your shirt and that enormous crow came down and stole the soap!'

The Mulla was completely unruffled. 'Look at the colour of my shirt, and look at the garment of a crow. His need was undoubtedly greater than mine. It is as well that he was able to obtain soap, even at my expense.'

Caught

The King sent a private mission around the countryside to find a modest man who could be appointed a judge. Nasrudin got wind of it.

When the delegation, posing as travellers, called on him, they found that he had a fishing-net draped over his shoulders.

'Why, pray,' one of them asked, 'do you wear that net?'

'Merely to remind myself of my humble origins, for I was once a fisherman.'

Nasrudin was appointed judge on the strength of this noble sentiment.

Visiting his court one day, one of the officials who had first seen him asked: "What happened to your net, Nasrudin?"

'There is no need of a net, surely,' said the Mulla-Judge, 'once the fish has been caught.'

But for the Grace ...

Seeing a white shape in the garden in the half-light, Nasrudin asked his wife to hand him his bow and arrows. He hit the object, went out to see what it was, came back almost in a state of collapse.

'That was a narrow shave. Just think. If I had been in that shirt of mine hanging there to dry, I would have been killed. It was shot right through the heart.'

Takes after his Father

Some of the Mulla's toddlers were playing around the house, and someone asked his small son:

'What is an aubergine?'

The son-and-heir immediately replied: 'A mauve calf which has not yet opened its eyes.'

Delirious with delight the Mulla gathered him up in his arms and kissed his head and feet.

'Did you hear that? Just like his father! AND I never told him—he made it up by himself!'

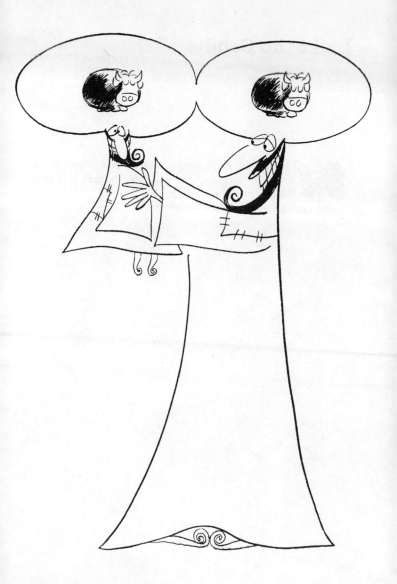

Light the Candle

Nasrudin was sitting talking with a friend as dusk fell.
'Light a candle,' the man said, 'because it is dark now. There is one just by your left side.'

'How can I tell my right from my left in the dark, you fool?' asked the Mulla.

Learning the hard Way

If you tell a person something in so many words, it will as like as not slide off him and will not be absorbed. Practical methods are essential.

A fakir called Nasrudin down from the roof of his house on which he was working. When the Mulla got to the ground the man said: 'Give me alms.'

'Why did you not call up to me?' asked the Mulla.

'I was ashamed,' said the man.

'Don't have false pride,' said Nasrudin, 'come up to the roof.'

As soon as they got to the top of the house and Nasrudin had started his work again, he said to the man, 'No, I have no alms for you.'

Something fell

Nasrudin's wife ran to his room when she heard a tremendous thump.

'Nothing to worry about,' said the Mulla, 'it was only my cloak which fell to the ground.'

'What, and made a noise like that?'

'Yes, I was inside it at the time.'

The Last Day

Nasrudin's neighbours coveted his fatted lamb, and often tried to make him kill it for a feast. Plan after plan failed until one day when they convinced him that within twenty-four hours the end of the world would come. 'In that case,' said the Mulla, 'we might as well eat it.'

So they had a feast.

When they had eaten, they lay down to sleep, taking off their jackets. After several hours the guests awoke to find that Nasrudin had piled all the clothes on a bonfire and burnt the lot.

They raised a howl of rage, but Nasrudin was calm: 'My brothers, tomorrow is the end of the world, remember? What need will you have of your clothes then?'

I'll take the Nine

n a dream Nasrudin saw himself being counted out coins. When there were nine silver pieces in his hand, the invisible donor stopped giving them.

Nasrudin shouted, 'I must have ten!' so loudly that he woke himself up.

Finding that all the money had disappeared he closed his eyes again and murmured, 'All right, then, give them back – I'll take the nine.'

He knows the Answer

A Turkoman's bull broke down Nasrudin's fence, and ran back to its owner. Nasrudin followed it and started to lash it.

'How dare you whip my bull!' roared the wild Turkoman.

'Never mind about that, you,' said Nasrudin; '*he* knows about it. The matter is between the two of us.'

What a Bird should look like

Nasrudin found a weary falcon sitting one day on his window-sill.

He had never seen a bird of this kind before.

'You poor thing,' he said, 'how ever were you allowed to get into this state?'

He clipped the falcon's talons and cut its beak straight, and trimmed its feathers.

'Now you look more like a bird,' said Nasrudin.

The Veil

t was the Mulla's wedding day. The marriage had been arranged, and he had never seen his wife's face. After the ceremony, when she removed her veil, he realized that she was terribly ugly.

While he was still stunned from this shock, she asked him:

'Now tell me, my love, your commands. In front of whom shall I remain veiled, and to whom shall I be allowed to show my face?'

'Show your face to anyone you like,' groaned the Mulla, 'as long as you don't show it to me.'

Your poor old Mother

Nasrudin's wife, angry with the Mulla for some reason, brought his soup boiling hot, hoping that he would scald his mouth with it. As soon as it was on the table she forgot and took a gulp herself without cooling it. Tears came to her eyes — but she still hoped that the Mulla would drink some of the boiling soup.

'Why are you crying?' he asked her.

'My poor old mother, just before she died, had some soup like this. The memory made me weep.'

Nasrudin turned to his soup and took a burning mouthful. Tears were soon coursing down his cheeks as well.

'Why, Nasrudin, surely you are not crying?'

'Yes,' said the Mulla, 'I am crying at the thought that your poor old mother died and left you alive.'

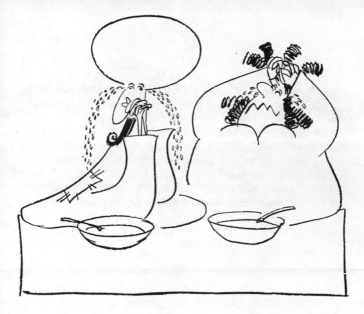

I know her best

eople ran to tell the Mulla that his mother-in-law had fallen into the river. 'She will be swept out to sea, for the torrent is very fast here,' they cried.

Without a moment's hesitation Nasrudin dived into the river and started to swim upstream.

'No!' they cried, '*downstream!* That is the only way a person can be carried away from here.'

'Listen!' panted the Mulla, 'I know my wife's mother. If everyone else is swept downstream, the place to look for *her* is upstream.'

The Secret

A would-be disciple haunted Nasrudin, asking him question after question. The Mulla answered everything, and realized that the man was not completely satisfied: although he was in fact making progress.

Eventually the man said: 'Master, I need more explicit guidance.'

'What is the matter?'

'I have to keep on doing things; and although I progress, I want to move faster. Please tell me a secret, as I have heard you do with others.'

'I will tell you when you are ready for it.'

The man later returned to the same theme.

'Very well. You know that your need is to emulate me?'

'Yes.'

'Can you keep a secret?'

'I would never impart it to anyone.'

'Then observe that I can keep a secret as well as you can.'

Do not disturb the Camels

asrudin was wandering in a graveyard. He stumbled and fell into an old grave. Beginning to visualize how it would feel if he were dead, he heard a noise. It flashed into his mind that the Angel of Reckoning was coming for him: though it was only a camel caravan passing by.

The Mulla jumped up and fell over a wall, stampeding several camels. The camelteers beat him with sticks.

He ran home in a distressed state. His wife asked him what the matter was, and why he was late.

'I have been dead,' said the Mulla.

Interested in spite of herself, she asked him what it was like.

'Not bad at all, unless you disturb the camels. Then they beat you.'

Happiness is not where you seek it

asrudin saw a man sitting disconsolately at the way-side, and asked what ailed him.

'There is nothing of interest in life, brother,' said the man; 'I have sufficient capital not to have to work, and I am on this trip only in order to seek something more interesting than the life I have at home. So far I haven't found it.'

Without another word, Nasrudin seized the traveller's knapsack and made off down the road with it, running like a hare. Since he knew the area, he was able to out-distance him.

The road curved, and Nasrudin cut across several loops, with the result that he was soon back on the road ahead of the man whom he had robbed. He put the bag by the side of the road and waited in concealment for the other to catch up.

Presently the miserable traveller appeared, following the tortuous road, more unhappy than ever because of his loss. As soon as he saw his property lying there, he ran towards it, shouting with joy.

'That's one way of producing happiness,' said Nasrudin.

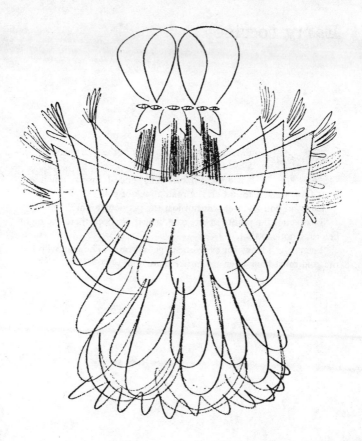

Early to rise

'Nasrudin, my son, get up early in the mornings.'

'Why, Father?'

'It is a good habit. Why, once I rose at dawn and went for a walk. I found on the road a sack of gold.'

'How did you know it was not lost the previous night?'

'That is not the point. In any case, it had not been there the night before. I noticed that.'

'Then it isn't lucky for everyone to get up early. The man who lost the gold must have been up earlier than you.'

The Majesty of the Sea

Regally the waves were hurling themselves upon the rocks, each deep-blue curve crested by whitest foam. Seeing this sight for the first time, Nasrudin was momentarily overwhelmed.

Then he went near to the seashore, took a little water in his cupped hand and tasted it.

'Why,' said the Mulla, 'to think that something with such pretensions is not worth drinking.'

Moment in Time

'What is Fate?' Nasrudin was asked by a scholar.

'An endless succession of intertwined events, each influencing the other.'

'That is hardly a satisfactory answer. I believe in cause and effect.'

'Very well,' said the Mulla, 'look at that.' He pointed to a procession passing in the street.

'That man is being taken to be hanged. Is that because someone gave him a silver piece and enabled him to buy the knife with which he committed the murder; or because someone saw him do it; or because nobody stopped him?'

Division of Labour

A ship, on which the Mulla was the only passenger, was caught in a typhoon. The captain and crew, having done all they could to save the ship, fell on their knees and started to pray for deliverance.

The Mulla stood calmly by.

The captain opened his eyes, saw the Mulla standing there, jumped up and cried: 'Get down on your knees! You, a devout man, you should be praying with us.'

Nasrudin did not move. 'I am only a passenger. Everything pertaining to the safety of this ship is your concern, not mine.'

You can't be too careful

The Mulla's wife had a friend, and she often used to give her food which Nasrudin had brought home for supper. One day he said: 'How is it that I bring home food and I never seem to see it?'

'The cat steals it.'

Nasrudin ran to get his axe and began to lock it in a chest.

'Why are you doing that?' his wife asked.

'I am hiding it,' said the Mulla; 'because if the cat can steal a pennyworth of meat, he is not likely to overlook an axe worth ten times that amount.'

All I needed was Time

The Mulla bought a donkey. Someone told him that he would have to give it a certain amount of food every day. This he considered to be too much. He would experiment, he decided, to get it used to less food. Each day, therefore, he reduced its rations.

Eventually, when the donkey was reduced to almost no food at all, it fell over and died.

'Pity,' said the Mulla. 'If I had had a little more time before it died I could have got it accustomed to living on nothing at all.'

Cut down on your Harness Intake

Visiting a sick friend, Nasrudin was just in time to see the doctor arrive. The man was in the house for less than a minute, and the speed of his diagnosis stunned the Mulla.

First the doctor looked at the patient's tongue, then he paused briefly. Then he said, 'You have been eating green apples. Stop doing this. You will be well in a couple of days.'

Forgetting everything else the Mulla pursued the doctor out of the house. 'Tell me, Doctor,' he panted, 'please tell me how you do it.'

'It was quite simple, when you have experience to distinguish various situations,' said the doctor. 'You see, as soon as I knew that the man had a stomach-ache, I looked for a cause. When I got into the sick-room, I saw a heap of green apple cores under the man's bed. The rest was obvious.'

Nasrudin thanked him for the lesson.

The next time he was visiting a friend it happened that the man's wife answered the door. 'Mulla,' she said, 'we don't need a philosopher, we need a doctor. My husband has a stomach-ache.'

'Don't think that the philosopher cannot be a physician, Madam,' said Nasrudin, forcing himself into the presence of the patient.

The sick man lay groaning on a bed. Nasrudin went straight to it, looked underneath, and called the wife into the room.

'Nothing serious,' he said; 'he will be well in a couple of days. But you must make sure that he cuts down on this habit of eating saddles and bridles.'

At Court

asrudin appeared at Court one day with a magnificent turban on his head.

He knew that the King would admire it, and that as a consequence he might be able to sell it to him.

'How much did you pay for that wonderful turban, Mulla?' the King asked.

'A thousand gold pieces, Majesty.'

A Vizier who saw what the Mulla was trying to do whispered to the King, 'Only a fool would pay that much for a turban.'

The King said: 'Why ever did you pay that amount? I have never heard of a turban at a thousand gold pieces.'

'Ah, Your Majesty, I paid it because I knew that there was in the whole world only one king who would buy such a thing.'

The King ordered Nasrudin to be given two thousand pieces of gold, and took the turban, pleased by the compliment.

'You may know the value of turbans,' the Mulla told the Vizier later, 'but I know the weaknesses of kings.'

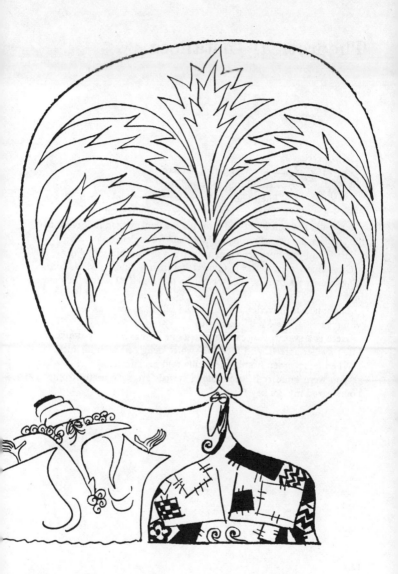

Theoretical Instances

'Where are you going, Mulla?'

'I am riding to town.'

'Then you had better leave your donkey behind, for there are robbers on the road, and someone might steal it.'

Nasrudin thought it was safer to ride his donkey than to leave it in the stable at home, where it might equally be stolen.

His friend therefore lent him a sword to defend himself with.

On a lonely part of the road he saw a man walking towards him. 'This must be a bandit,' said Nasrudin to himself. 'I will anticipate him.'

The innocent traveller was surprised when, as soon as they were within earshot, the Mulla called out:

'Here is a sword, you can have it. Now let me keep my donkey.' The traveller agreed, and took the sword, delighted with his luck.

When he returned home, the Mulla told his friend:

'You were quite right, you know, swords are very useful things. Yours saved my donkey for me.'

The Pace of Life

'Why can't we move faster?' Nasrudin's employer asked him one day. 'Every time I ask you to do something, you do it piecemeal. There is really no need to go to the market three times to buy three eggs.'

Nasrudin promised to reform.

His master fell ill. 'Call the doctor, Nasrudin.'

The Mulla went out and returned, together with a horde of people. 'Here, master, is the doctor. And I have brought the others as well.'

'Who are all the others?'

'If the doctor should order a poultice, I have brought the poultice-maker, his assistant and the men who supply the ingredients, in case we need many poultices. The coalman is here to see how much coal we might need to heat water to make poultices. Then there is the undertaker, in case you do not survive.'

The Sample

Sitting one day in the teahouse, Nasrudin was impressed by the rhetoric of a travelling scholar. Questioned by one of the company on some point, the sage drew a book from his pocket and banged it on the table: 'This is my evidence! *And* I wrote it myself.'

A man who could not only read but write was a rarity. And a man who had written a book! The villagers treated the pedant with profound respect.

Some days later Mulla Nasrudin appeared at the teahouse and asked whether anyone wanted to buy a house.

'Tell us something about it, Mulla,' the people asked him, 'for we did not even know that you had a house of your own.'

'Actions speak louder than words!' shouted Nasrudin.

From his pocket he took a brick, and hurled it on the table in front of him.

'This is my evidence. Examine it for quality. *And* I built the house myself.'

Other People's Mail

Nasrudin could not write very well. His reading ability was even poorer. But he was more literate than the other villagers; and one day he agreed to take down a letter from a yokel to his brother.

'Now read it back to me,' said the man, 'because I want to make sure that I have not left anything out.'

The Mulla peered at the scrawl. Finding that he could not get further than 'My dear Brother,' he said:

'I cannot quite make it out. I am not sure if the next words are "know" or "work", and "before" or "heart".

'But this is terrible. Who is going to read it if *you* can't?'

'My good man,' said Nasrudin, 'that is not *my* problem. My job is to write the letter, not to read it.'

'Besides,' agreed the villager, completely convinced, 'it is not addressed to you, is it?'

Why didn't you tell me before?

Nasrudin and a disciple were on the road. Whenever they arrived at a large house, they would present themselves, in the manner of travelling dervishes, at the door. Food would be handed to them, and also water.

Nasrudin used to eat as much as he could, then lie down to sleep. The disciple ate a little, then shook himself, then ate more.

After some days the Mulla asked him why he ate in such a strange manner.

'Well, Master, I find that if I eat a little, then drink some water then settle it all by shaking, I can hold more.'

Nasrudin took off his sandal and gave the youth a couple of blows:

'How dare you conceal such a valuable secret from me! Oh, to think of the amount of food I have wasted by not being able to eat it! I knew that the limit of eating must be farther ahead than I could attain. The limit of filling is, after all, bursting.'

Supply and Demand

His Imperial Majesty the Shahinshah arrived unexpectedly at the teahouse where Nasrudin had been left in charge.

The Emperor called for an omelette.

'We shall now continue with the hunt,' he told the Mulla. 'So tell me what I owe you.'

'For you and your five companions, Sire, the omelettes will be a thousand gold pieces.'

The Emperor raised his eyebrows.

'Eggs must be very costly here. Are they as scarce as that?'

'It is not the eggs which are scarce here, Majesty — it is the visits of kings.'

The Value of the Past

Nasrudin was sent by the King to investigate the lore of various kinds of Eastern mystical teachers. They all recounted to him tales of the miracles and the sayings of the founders and great teachers, all long dead, of their schools.

When he returned home, he submitted his report, which contained the single word 'Carrots'.

He was called upon to explain himself. Nasrudin told the King: 'The best part is buried; few know—except the farmer—by the green that there is orange underground; if you don't work for it, it will deteriorate; there are a great many donkeys associated with it.'

Aplomb

asrudin and a friend went to an eating-house and decided, for the sake of economy, to share a plate of aubergines.

They argued violently as to whether they should be stuffed or fried.

Tired and hungry, Nasrudin yielded and the order was given for stuffed aubergines.

His companion suddenly collapsed as they were waiting, and seemed in a bad way. Nasrudin jumped up.

'Are you going for a doctor?' asked someone at the next table.

'No, you fool,' shouted Nasrudin. 'I am going to see whether it is too late to change the order.'

Kinds of Day

A man stopped Nasrudin and asked him what day of the week it was.

'Couldn't tell you,' said the Mulla. 'I am a stranger in these parts. I don't know what days of the week they have here.'

Alone in the Desert

Nasrudin was wandering along a desert track, when he met three fierce Arabs.

They had been arguing.

'There are three possibilities as to how minarets could have come about,' they said. 'We have just heard of them, and are wondering which is the correct one.'

Nasrudin was not sure. 'Tell me your theories, and I will judge,' he said.

'They fell from heaven,' said the first.

'They were built in a well and then hoisted up,' said the second.

'They grew like cacti,' said the third.

Each man drew a knife to reinforce his version.

Nasrudin said: 'You are all wrong. They were built by giants of olden times, who had a longer reach than ours.'

Maiden in Distress

Nasrudin was strolling one summer evening past a walled garden, and decided to look over at what delights might be within. He climbed the wall, and saw a beautiful maiden in the embrace of a hideous monster, a deformed apparition, as it seemed to him.

Without a second's pause the chivalrous Nasrudin leapt into the garden and put the beast to flight with a series of blows and curses.

As he turned back to receive the lady's thanks, she struck him in the eye. Two enormous servants seized the Mulla and threw him back into the street, and then belaboured him.

As he lay there, half insensible, he heard the woman crying hysterically for her lover, whom Nasrudin had frightened away.

'There is no accounting for tastes,' said Nasrudin. After that he cultivated a limp and wore an eye-patch, but no maiden called him into her garden during his walks.

Unfair

Nasrudin walked into the city of Konia for the first time. He was at once struck by the number of pâtisseries. His appetite sharpened, he went into one of these shops and started to devour a pie.

Certain that he would get nothing out of this ragged apparition, the owner rushed at him and cuffed him.

'What kind of a town is this?' asked the Mulla; 'a place where they hit a man as soon as he has started eating.'

What has gone before ...

n a dark alleyway an agile pickpocket tried to snatch Nasrudin's purse. The Mulla was too quick for him, and there was a violent struggle. Eventually Nasrudin got his man down on the ground.

At this moment a charitable woman passing called out:

'You bully! Let that little man get up, and give him a chance.'

'Madam,' panted Nasrudin, 'you ignore the trouble which I have had getting him down.'

All you need

'I'll have you hanged,' said a cruel and ignorant king, who had heard of Nasrudin's powers, 'if you don't prove that you are a mystic.'

'I see strange things,' said Nasrudin at once; 'a golden bird in the sky, demons under the earth.'

'How can you see through solid objects? How can you see far into the sky?'

'Fear is all you need.'

Why are we waiting?

hree thousand distinguished epicures had been invited to a feast at the Caliph's palace in Baghdad. Nasrudin, by some mistake, was among them.

This was an annual event, and each year the main dish excelled that of the previous feast, because the Caliphial reputation for magnificence had to be sustained and excelled.

But Nasrudin had come only for the food.

After a long wait, preparatory ceremonies, singing and dancing, an enormous number of huge silver dishes were carried in. On each one, placed between five guests, was a whole roasted peacock, decorated with artificial but edible wings and beak, its plumage shining with sugary precious gems.

There was a gasp of delight from the gourmets at Nasrudin's table, as they feasted their eyes on this supreme work of creative art.

Nobody seemed to be making any move towards the food.

The Mulla was starving. Suddenly he jumped up and bellowed:

'All right! I admit it does look strange. But it is probably food. Let us eat it before it eats us!'

The Flood

'The King has been kind to me,' a man was telling Nasrudin; 'I planted wheat and the rains came. He heard of my troubles and compensated me for the damage done by the flood.'

The Mulla thought for a moment.

'Tell me,' he asked, 'how does one *cause* a flood?'

The Omen

The King was in a bad mood. As he left the palace to go hunting he saw Nasrudin.

'It is bad luck to see a Mulla on the way to a hunt,' he shouted to his guards. 'Don't let him stare at me — whip him out of the way!'

They did so.

As it happened, the chase was successful.

The King sent for Nasrudin.

'I am sorry, Mulla. I thought you were a bad omen. You were not, it transpires.'

'YOU thought *I* was a bad omen!' said Nasrudin. 'YOU look at *me* and get a full game-bag. *I* look at YOU, and I get a whipping. Who is a bad omen for whom?'

Turnips are harder

The Mulla one day decided to take the King some fine turnips which he had grown.

On the way he met a friend, who advised him to present something more refined, such as figs or olives.

He bought some figs, and the King, who was in a good humour, accepted them and rewarded him.

Next week he bought some huge oranges and took them to the palace. But the King was in a bad temper, and threw them at Nasrudin, bruising him.

As he picked himself up, the Mulla realized the truth. 'Now I understand,' he said; 'people take smaller things rather than heavy ones because when you are pelted it does not hurt so much. If it had been those turnips, I would have been killed.'

How Nasrudin spoke up

Nasrudin said:

'One day a marvellous horse was brought before the prince at whose Court I sat. Nobody could ride it, because it was far too mettlesome a steed. Suddenly, in the heat of my pride and chivalry I cried out:

' "None of you dare to ride this splendid horse; none of you! None of you can stay on his back!" And I sprang forward.'

Someone asked: 'What happened?'

'I couldn't ride it either,' said the Mulla.

In the midst of Life

Nasrudin was preaching in a mosque at the time of the Tatar conquest of Western Asia. He was no supporter of Tamerlane.

Tamerlane had heard that the Mulla was against him, and crept into the mosque dressed as a dervish.

'God will strike the Tatars,' Nasrudin announced at the end of his sermon.

'He will not grant your prayer,' said the dervish, stepping forward.

'And why not?' asked Nasrudin.

'Because you are being punished for what you have done and what you have not done. There is such a thing as cause and effect. How can anyone be punished for doing something which is itself a chastisement?'

Nasrudin began to feel uncomfortable; for dervishes are not to be trifled with.

'Who are you, and what is your name?' he asked, blustering a little.

'I am a dervish, and my name is Timur.'

A number of the congregation now rose, bows and arrows in their hands. They were disguised members of the Tatar horde.

Nasrudin took it all in with a glance.

'Does your name end in "Lame" by any chance?'

'It does,' said the dervish.

Nasrudin turned to the congregation, who were petrified with fear:

'Brethren, we have performed a congregational prayer. Now we shall start the congregational funeral service.'

Timur the Lame was so amused that he dismissed the troops and asked Nasrudin to join his Court.

Awake or Asleep?

One day Nasrudin noticed that a wonderful new road—a *Shah-Rah*, or 'King's Highway'—had been built at some distance from his house. 'This is something which I must try out,' he thought.

He walked along the road for a long time, when sleep overcame him. When he woke up, he found that his turban was missing—someone had stolen it.

The next day he started along the road again, hoping to find some trace of the thief. He walked for several miles in the summer heat, and again composed himself to sleep for a while.

He was woken by a clatter of hooves and a jingle of harness. A posse was approaching: fierce-looking soldiers of the King's Guard, escorting a prisoner. Overcome by curiosity he stopped them and asked what was going on.

'We are taking this man to be beheaded,' said the captain, 'for he is a guard placed on this road, whom we found asleep.'

'That is enough for me,' said Nasrudin. 'You can keep your road. Whoever falls asleep on it loses either his hat or his head. Who knows what the third loss might be?'

And this is the origin of the Persian proverb: 'Whoever falls asleep on the highway loses either his hat or his head.'

Presently Nasrudin felt his wife shaking him. 'Wake up,' she said.

'That's torn it,' groaned the Mulla. 'What you call "awake" I call "asleep".'

The Short Cut

Walking home one wonderful morning, Nasrudin thought that it would be a good idea to take a short cut through the woods. 'Why', he asked himself, 'should I plod along a dusty road when I could be communing with Nature, listening to the birds and looking at the flowers? This is indeed a day of days; a day for fortunate pursuits!'

So saying, he launched himself into the greenery. He had not gone very far, however, when he fell into a pit, where he lay reflecting.

'It is not such a fortunate day, after all,' he meditated; 'in fact it is just as well that I took this short cut. If things like this can happen in a beautiful setting like this, what might not have befallen me on that nasty highway?'

Change the Subject

One sweltering afternoon, Nasrudin saw a man walking along the dusty road towards him, carrying a big bunch of luscious-looking grapes.

A little flattery might be worth a grape.

'O great Sheikh – give me a few grapes,' said Nasrudin.

'I am not a sheikh,' said the dervish, for he was one of those travelling contemplatives who shunned any extreme form of speech.

'He is a man of even greater importance, and I have slighted him,' thought the Mulla. Aloud he said:

'*Walahadrat-a!* (Highness) – give me just one grape!'

'I am *not* a Highness!' snarled the dervish.

'Well, don't tell me what you are, or we will probably find out that those are not grapes, either! Let's change the subject.'

The Rope and the Sky

A Sufi mystic stopped Nasrudin in the street. In order to test whether the Mulla was sensitive to inner knowledge, he made a sign, pointing at the sky.

The Sufi meant, 'There is only one truth, which covers all.'

Nasrudin's companion, an ordinary man, thought: 'The Sufi is mad. I wonder what precautions Nasrudin will take?'

Nasrudin looked in a knapsack and took out a coil of rope. This he handed to his companion.

'Excellent,' thought the companion, 'we will bind him up if he becomes violent.'

The Sufi saw that Nasrudin meant: 'Ordinary humanity tries to find truth by methods as unsuitable as attempting to climb into the sky with a rope.'

Who am I?

After a long journey, Nasrudin found himself amid the milling throng in Baghdad. This was the biggest place he had ever seen, and the people pouring through the streets confused him.

'I wonder how people manage to keep track of themselves, who they are, in a place like this,' he mused.

Then he thought, 'I must remember myself well, otherwise I might lose myself.'

He rushed to a caravanserai. A wag was sitting on his bed, next to the one which Nasrudin was allotted. Nasrudin thought he would have a siesta, but he had a problem: how to find himself again when he woke up.

He confided in his neighbour.

'Simple,' said the joker. 'Here is an inflated bladder. Tie it around your leg and go to sleep. When you wake up, look for the man with the balloon, and that will be you.'

'Excellent idea,' said Nasrudin.

A couple of hours later, the Mulla awoke. He looked for the bladder, and found it tied to the leg of the wag. 'Yes, that is me,' he thought. Then, in a frenzy of fear he started pummelling the other man: 'Wake up! Something has happened, as I thought it would! Your idea was no good!'

The man woke up and asked him what the trouble was. Nasrudin pointed to the bladder. 'I can tell by the bladder that *you* are *me*. But if *you* are *me* – who, for the love of goodness, AM I?'

I'd have shown you

'Some people', said the Mulla to himself one day, 'are dead when they seem to be alive. Others, again, are alive although they seem to be dead. How can we tell if a man is dead or if he is alive?'

He repeated this last sentence so loudly that his wife heard. She said to him: 'Foolish man! If the hands and feet are quite cold, you can be sure that he is dead.'

Not long afterwards Nasrudin was cutting wood in the forest when he realized that his extremities were almost frozen by the bitter cold.

'Death', he said, 'now seems to be upon me. The dead do not cut wood; they lie down respectably, for they have no need of physical movement.'

He lay down under a tree.

A pack of wolves, emboldened by their sufferings during that harsh winter, and thinking the man dead, descended upon the Mulla's donkey and ate it.

'Such is life!' the Mulla reflected; 'one thing is conditional upon another. Had I been alive you would not have taken such liberties with my donkey.'

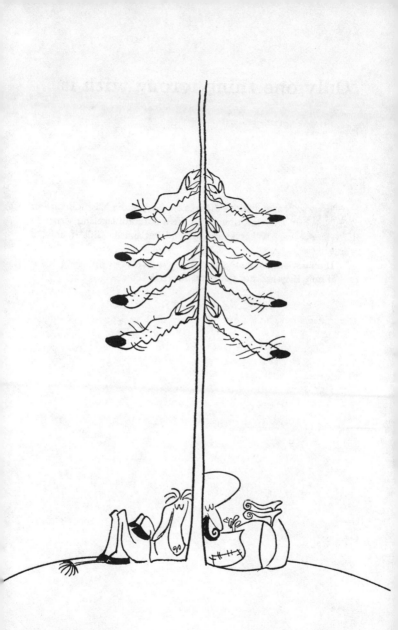

Only one thing wrong with it

Walking with a disciple one day, Mulla Nasrudin saw for the first time in his life a beautiful lakeland scene.

'What a delight!' he exclaimed. 'But if only, if only ...'

'If only what, Master?'

'If only they had not put water into it!'

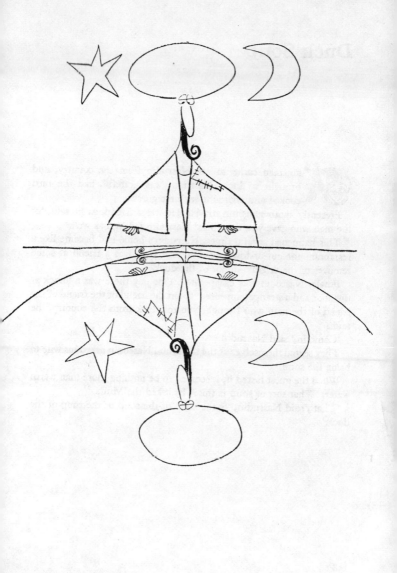

Duck Soup

A kinsman came to see Nasrudin from the country, and brought a duck. Nasrudin was grateful, had the bird cooked and shared it with his guest.

Presently another visitor arrived. He was a friend, as he said, 'of the man who gave you the duck.' Nasrudin fed him as well.

This happened several times. Nasrudin's home had become like a restaurant for out-of-town visitors. Everyone was a friend at some removes of the original donor of the duck.

Finally Nasrudin was exasperated. One day there was a knock at the door and a stranger appeared. 'I am the friend of the friend of the friend of the man who brought you the duck from the country,' he said.

'Come in,' said Nasrudin.

They seated themselves at the table, and Nasrudin asked his wife to bring the soup.

When the guest tasted it, it seemed to be nothing more than warm water. 'What sort of soup is this?' he asked the Mulla.

'That', said Nasrudin, 'is the soup of the soup of the soup of the duck.'

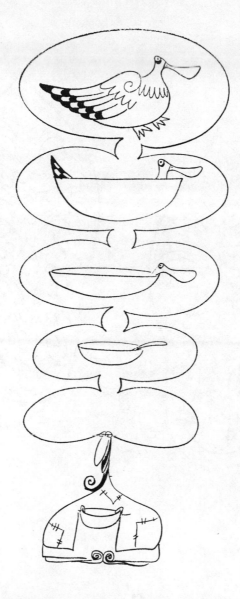

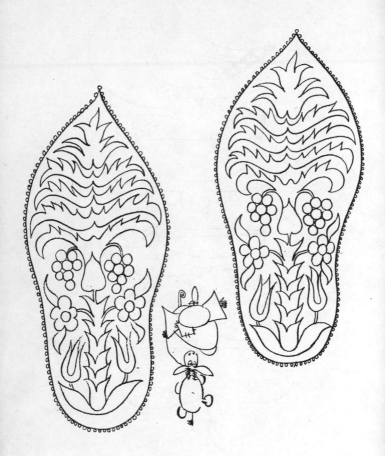